P. W. Raidabaugh

History of the English Bible

Text-Book No. 8

P. W. Raidabaugh

History of the English Bible
Text-Book No. 8

ISBN/EAN: 9783743398740

Manufactured in Europe, USA, Canada, Australia, Japa

Cover: Foto ©ninafisch / pixelio.de

Manufactured and distributed by brebook publishing software (www.brebook.com)

P. W. Raidabaugh

History of the English Bible

EVANGELICAL NORMAL SERIES.

———•———

TEXT-BOOK No. 8.

———

HISTORY

OF THE

ENGLISH BIBLE.

COMPILED AND EDITED BY

P. W. RAIDABAUGH.

———•———

CLEVELAND, O.
Publishing House of the Evangelical Association,
LAUER & YOST, Agents.
1885.

Entered, according to act of Congress, in the year 1885,
By LAUER & YOST,
In the Office of the Librarian of Congress, at Washington.

PREFACE.

The Bible is a revelation of God's will to man, and was originally written in the Hebrew and Greek languages, with several small portions in Chaldee. It is the oldest book extant. Its earliest pages were written three thousand years before the invention of printing; it ante-dates the writings of Confucius and all other ancient writings. Through all the ages it was necessary to write copies of the Bible, which was attended with much labor, and made the price of a copy so high that but few were written.

It is not the object of this book to give a history of how the Bible was made in the different languages; neither is it the object to give the trials and difficulties of preserving the Word of God among men. It has a single purpose — to give a condensed history of the ENGLISH TRANSLATIONS of the Bible.

In compiling this volume, the author is indebted for many facts to "Our English Bible," published by the London Tract Society; "Annals of the Bible"; "Bagster's Hexapla," and "How the Bible was made," by E. M. Wood, D. D.

That it may be helpful in creating a proper appreciation of the Word of God in the English language, is the prayer of the writer.

P. W. R.

Cleveland, O., August, 1884.

HISTORY OF THE ENGLISH BIBLE.

INTRODUCTORY CHAPTER.

The principal translations of the Scriptures previous to the first printed English Bible were:

1. THE SEPTUAGINT.

This was the most important Greek translation of the Old Testament, and the oldest in any language. It was made in Alexandria, Egypt, in the third century before Christ. In the third century, after Christ, Origen made a careful revision of the Septuagint. It was first printed in 1518 at Venice, Italy.

2. ARAMIC.

About the time of Christ there was made a translation of the Pentateuch, from Hebrew into Aramic, for the benefit of those Jews, who were more familiar with the Aramic, or Chaldee language. Afterward other parts of the Old Testament were also translated into the Aramic. These translations were called *Targums*. They are ten in number, the most important being the "Targum of Onkelas." It was also first printed at Venice, in 1609.

3. Syriac.

About the second century after Christ the Jews, who had accepted the Christian faith, translated the Scriptures into the Syriac language. This version is called "The Peshito."

4. Latin.

The most renowned Latin versions of the Scriptures are the "Vetus Latina," and the "Vulgate."

The "Vetus Latina" was translated from the Septuagint, and supposed to have been made in Africa about the second century after Christ. In the fourth century Jerome revised it; but it was not satisfactory to him, so he made a new translation from the original Hebrew. This is called the "Vulgate." It has had several revisions, by direction of different Popes, and is the standard Bible of the Church of Rome. It was first printed at Mentz, by Guttenberg, somewhere between 1450 and 1455. It was the first book printed from movable type.

5. German.

There were small portions of the Bible translated into the German language, between the ninth and fourteenth centuries. About the year 1466 a translation was made from the "Vulgate," and printed at Strassburg, this was followed by four other editions during the next eleven years. Between 1477 and 1522 nine other editions followed.

In 1522 Luther's New Testament was published at Wittenberg, in two volumes. In 1524 the whole Bible, with the exception of the prophetical books, translated by Luther from the original languages, was published at Nuremberg. It appeared in three folio volumes.

6. OTHER TRANSLATIONS.

The following were translations from the "Vulgate," and printed as follows :

>Italian, 1471, at Venice.
>Flemish, 1475, at Cologne.
>Spanish, 1478, at Valencia.
>French, 1487, at Paris.
>Bohemian, 1488, at Prague.

The first Polyglot Bible was published by Cardinal Ximenes. It was begun in 1502, and was printed in six volumes — between 1514 and 1517, but did not appear until 1522, and then but six hundred copies were printed. It was printed at Alcala, in Spain. The Old Testament had the Hebrew, Latin, and Greek in three columns, and a Chaldee paraphrase at the bottom of the page. The New Testament had the Greek and Latin in parallel columns.

CHAPTER I.

EARLY SAXON TRANSLATIONS.

The earliest attempt at a Saxon translation of the Scriptures, with which we are acquainted, has generally been ascribed to Cædmon, a monk of Whitby, in the seventh century. The work, however, for the most part, is a diffuse poetic paraphrase, which he entitled the "Origin of Things." "The Old Testament," observes Mr. Wright in his Superstitions of England, "was fertile in subjects which were agreeable to the feelings of Saxons, wars and heroic deeds, and some poet stringing together a few of the better poems on Scripture subjects, by very unequal verses of his own, has formed a kind of poetic version of the Bible which is preserved in a very mutilated state in a manuscript at Oxford, and which has been twice printed under the name of Cædmon." The inequality of the different parts of the poem attributed to Cædmon was first noticed by Conybeare. A fine poem on the Fall of the Angels, the Creation, and the Fall of Man, is awkwardly prefaced by a narration of the same story much more briefly told. Then we have a barren version of the chapters of Genesis to the close of the life of Abraham, except the accounts of the flood and of the war of the kings against Sodom, which are told in a superior style. Suddenly, without any connexion with that of Abraham, we are introduced to the history of Moses, which again is told in a very different manner, and has all the marks of being a separate poem. After the history of Moses, follows that of Nebuchadnezzar, equally distinct and complete in itself, which occupies all the remainder of the first part. The second part comprises chiefly a poem on the descent of Christ into hades, a favorite story, known in somewhat later times as the harrowing of hell.

In the century following, that in which Cædmon flourished, two versions of the Psalter, in Saxon, are said to have been made, one by Aldhelm, bishop of Sherborne, and the other by Guthlac, the first Saxon ancharite.

Aldhelm was a monk, born at Wessex, 656, and, as bishop of Sherborne, he died in 709. He was an ascetic of strictest kind. He is said to have immersed himself to the shoulders, Winter and Summer, in a fountain near the abbey, and would not come forth until he had repeated the Psalter entirely. By his direction the first organ was built in England. He was the first Englishman who wrote in Latin, and he taught his people to compose Latin verses.

Guthlac was a monk at Repton, where he devoted himself especially to the study of the lives of the Hermits. He then retired to Cragland, a desolate island, where he is said to have made his translation of the Psalter. He died at the age of forty-seven years.

The earliest translations from the New Testament were executed by the venerable Bede, who was born in County Durham about 672, and died in 735, and spent his early life in the Monastery at Jarrow, and the remainder of his life in the Monastery at Wearmouth, and was president of both. He wrote much and translated into Anglo-Saxon the Lord's Prayer and the Apostle's Creed. He gives us the only reliable history of Saxon ecclesiastical matters of that age. He died immediately after finishing his translation of the Gospel of St. John. The scene, as given by an old monkish chronicle, is very touching. "There remains now only one chapter, but it seems difficult for you to speak," exclaims the scribe, as his pen traces on the parchment the last verse of the 20th chapter of John. "It is easy," replied Bede, "take your pen, dip it in ink, and write as fast as you can." "Now, master," says the monk, "now, only one sentence is wanting." Bede repeats it — "It is finished," says the scribe — "It is finished!" replied the dying saint; "lift up my head, let me sit in the cell, in the place where I have been accustomed to pray — and now glory be to the Father, and the Son, and the Holy Ghost." And with the utterance of these words, his spirit fled, whilst seated on the floor of his cell. It was, indeed, a noble distinction for Bede to die in the act of translating the Word of God.

The next attempt at an Anglo-Saxon translation from the Scriptures, of which we can discover any trace, may be found among the Cottonian manuscripts of the British Museum. It is a version in what is called the Durham Book, written between the lines of the Latin text of the four Gospels. The Latin was copied by Eadfrid, a monk of the bleak isle of Lindisfarne, in the time of the famous St. Cuthbert, whom he succeeded in the bishopric. He died in 687. The Anglo-Saxon version was made by one Aldred, a priest. Its age cannot be ascertained with any precision; but it probably belongs to the reign of king Alfred. It may interest the reader to peruse the following translation of the Lord's Prayer into the tongue spoken by our ancestors, and to trace in the rather uncouth-looking words some striking resemblance in sound to the language of the present day.

"Fader uren thu arth in heofnum, sie gehalgud noma thin: to cymeth ric thin; sie willo thin suæls inheofne & in eortho; hlaf useune ofer wistlic sel us todæg: & forgef us scylda usna suæ forgeofon scyldgum usum: & ne inlæd usih in costunge uh gefrig usich from yfle."

The old quarto volume, in which this translation is preserved, is one of the most beautiful specimens of penmanship we possess. One might almost fancy the letters were engraved. There are in the book many ornaments and pictures by St. Ethelwald, who succeeded Eadfurth in the see of Durham. It contains four curious portraits of the Evangelists, and the initial letter of each Gospel is finely illuminated.

After the Durham Book comes the Rushworth Gloss, a manuscript existing in the Bodleian Library. It is an interlineary Saxon translation of the Gospels, written about the same time as the former work. It has colored initials, and ornamental delineations of the Evangelists. The parties who executed the version have preserved their names — "Owen, that this book glossed, and Farmen, the priest, at Harewood." The copyist has also taken care to perpetuate his name in connexion with his labors, one Macreogol, who prays that the reader may not forget to intercede for the writer.

Alfred the Great, whose character and reign shine across the clouds of the dark ages like a brilliant gleam of light, who sought the moral and religious improvement, as well as the civilization of his people, engaged, in his latter days, upon a translation of the Psalms into the vernacular language, but was cut off by death in the midst of his useful task. Next in order come some fragments of an interlineary translation of Proverbs, so imperfect that here and there only one word in Saxon is placed over a whole line in Latin. These fragments are contained in a volume among the Cottonian archives of the British Museum.

In the reign of Ethelred, the monk Ælfric distinguished himself by his industry in this department of sacred literature. He wrote an epitome of the Old and New Testaments, and translated several historical books of the former. The Heptateuch, the Book of Job, the imperfect history of Judith, and the apocryphal Gospel of Nicodemus, in Ælfric's version, were published in the year 1698, by Edward Thwaites. The best of his translations are but very incorrect. Sometimes, indeed, he gives accurate renderings of passages, but commonly he substitutes paraphrases and statements of his own, expressing generally the sense of the original. In the library of Corpus Christi, Cambridge, there is a manuscript of the four Gospels, in Saxon, anterior to the conquest; and in the Bodleian is another copy of the same version. Good old John Fox published the volume, accompanied by an English version, rejoicing much that he could thus appeal to antiquity in favor of vernacular versions, then viewed with so much jealousy by the church of Rome.

During the period when the waves of Danish invasion successively swept over the shores of England and almost desolated some parts of their country, scarcely any efforts towards vernacular versions of the Word of God seem to have been made. A few manuscripts of the Psalms belonging to the latter end of the age of the Saxons are all that remain.

When William the Norman, England's second great conqueror, stepped on the shore, near Hastings, he came as the instrument of Providence to effect great changes in the language as well as the social habits and the general civilization of the Anglican races. A new dialect made its appearance. The old English tongue entered a transition state. It became mixed with words and inflections of Norman origin. A number of fragments of this age are found in museums and libraries; they consist not of translations, strictly speaking, but of poems — in some cases, paraphrases, in other cases, mere stories of Scriptural facts in verse. The first of these poetical compositions is entitled "Ormulum," because written by a person named Orme; and it consists of a very feeble history of the events described in the Gospels and Acts. We give John 1: 35-37 as a sample from this book:

> Thoerofften onn an others dagg
>   Stud Sannt Johan Bapptisste,
> Tneggen stodenn thaer withth himm
>   Off hire Learnimgenihhten,
> He sahh me Lafend than,
>   And seggde thuss withth worde;
> See here, thiss iss Goden Lamb.
>   To two Learnimgenihhten,
> Harrdenn thatt word, and gedenn forth
>   Affterward me Lafend.

The second of this class is the famous "Soulehele," in the huge Vernon MS. of the Bodleian, which, according to the best critics, belongs to the thirteenth century. The following lines, relative to the crucifixion, will give some idea of the nature of this Biblical poem:

"Our ladi and hire sustur stoden under the roode,
And seint John, with Marie Magdaleyn with wel sori moode,
Ur Ladi biheold hire sweete son ibrought in gret pyne,
I for monnes gultes nouthen her and nothing for myne,
Marie weop wel sore, and bitter teres leet,
The teres fullen uppon the ston doun at hire feet."

The third production of this kind, but in shorter measure, comprising the history of the facts in Genesis and Exodus, is found in the library of Corpus Christi, Cambridge. And the fourth metrical version, containing the Psalms, is preserved in the same collection; of which, however, a copy or revision — in some parts considerably altered — may be seen in the British Museum:

Corpus Christi Cant. First Psalm.
"Seli beern that nouht is zon,
In the red of wicked man,
And in strete of sinful nouth he stod,
Ne sat in sete of scorne ungode,
Both in lawe of Louerd his wille beay
And his lawe yinke he night and day."

The earliest of all English prose translations of Scripture, known to be in existence, is the work of Richard Rolle, an Augustinian eremite.

He lived in solitude, close by the convent of Hampole, a village about four miles from Doncaster; and there he carried on his studies, and wrote his works; he died in 1349. He is known in the annals of our literature as the author of several theological pieces in Latin, and especially of the " Prick of Conscience; " a curious old English poem, of which the reader may find ample specimens in Warton's History of English Poetry. His prose translation from the Scripture consists of the book of Psalms, of which several manuscripts are in existence — the one in Sidney College claiming to be the original. The following is a specimen of the manner in which the hermit fulfilled his task:

Sidney Manuscript. *Psalm* xxiii. 1-3.

Our lord governeth me nothynge to me shal wante, stede of pasture thar he me sette. In the water of the hetyng forth he me brougte; my soule he turnyde.

He ladde me on the stretis of rygtnisnesse: for his name.

For nin gif I hadde goo in myddil of the shadene of deeth; I shal not dreede yueles, for thou art with me.

Rolle, in his work of translation, was evidently bent upon doing good, and in a prologue to his book, he informs us, that he sought no strange English, but what was easiest and most common, that he followed the letter of the Latin text as far as possible, and that, in expounding it, he followed the holy doctors, and aimed at reproving sin. This, as he further observes, was stated in order to meet the objections of envious men, who might say that he did not understand what he was doing, and was thereby injuring himself and others. A short comment or gloss is inserted after each sentence, which, in the simplest manner, explains the meaning of the passage.

CHAPTER II.

WYCLIFFE AND HIS TRANSLATIONS.

John Wycliffe was born in the village of Wycliffe, Yorkshire, about 1324. He entered Oxford University, and there, in 1360, became noted as an opponent of the mendicant friars, and in 1366 took the degree of Doctor of Divinity, and died peacefully in 1384. His body was exhumed in 1428 and burned, and his ashes thrown in the river.

Wycliffe was appointed by Edward III. to the rectory of Lutterworth, about the year 1376, in part as a reward for his services at Bruges, whither he had gone as a commissioner with the bishop of Bangor, to negotiate with a papal embassy in that city respecting the reservation of benefices. That visit brought him better acquainted than before with the corruption of the Roman court, and roused his indignation against the papal system. Twenty years before he had written his tract, entitled "The Last Age of the Church," which showed that he then deplored the enormous ecclesiastical evils of the day. And in the controversy between Edward III. and the Pope, respecting the papal claim of tribute from England, he had fearlessly contended against the claim as unjust and arrogant. But now, on his return from Bruges, reviewing what he had there seen and heard, he came out as a more decided champion than ever for a reformation of the church. Indeed, so bold was the course he pursued, that, soon after his return, he was cited to appear at St. Paul's to answer certain charges against him, when a scene of tumult occurred, quaintly described by Foxe, which ended in the deliverance of Wycliffe from his enemies, through the interposition of his illustrious friend, John of Gaunt, duke of Lancaster. The Pope, however, would allow the reformer no peace, but despatched against him bull after bull; happily without effect, the refractory ecclesiastic enjoying the special favor and patronage of royalty.

All this excitement sharpened his love for the Holy Scriptures as the true standard of religious principles and ecclesiastical discipline. About this time it was that he wrote his book upon the Truth and Meaning of Scripture, in which he maintains that Christ's law is sufficient; "that a Christian man well understanding it may gather sufficient knowledge during his pilgrimage upon earth; that all truth is contained in Scripture; that we should admit of no conclusion not approved there; that there is no court beside the court of heaven; that though there were a hundred Popes, and all the friars in the world were turned into cardinals, yet should we learn more from the Gospel than we should from all that multitude; and that true sons will in no wise go about to infringe the will and testament of their heavenly Father."

It was about this time that Wycliffe began his translation. His writings subsequent to the year 1378 exhibit abundant arguments in support of the sufficiency of Scripture, and in defence of vernacular translations. "As the faith of the church," he says, "is contained in the Scriptures, the more these are known in an orthodox sense, the better. And since secular men should assuredly understand the faith, it should be taught them in whatever language is best known to them. Inasmuch also, as the doctrines of our faith are more clearly and precisely expressed in the Scriptures than they may possibly be by priests, seeing, if one may venture so to speak, that many prelates are but too ignorant of Scripture, and as the verbal instructions of priests have many other defects, the conclusion is abundantly plain that believers should ascertain for themselves the matters of their faith by having the Scriptures in a language which they fully understand. According to the constant doctrine of Augustine, the Scriptures contain the whole of truth, and this translation of them should therefore do at least this good, namely, placing bishops and priests above suspicion as to the parts of it which they profess to explain. Other means also, as prelates, the pope, and friars, may prove defective; and to provide against this, Christ and his apostles evangelized the greater portion of the world, by making known the Scriptures in a language which was familiar to the people. To this end, indeed, did the Holy Spirit endow them with the knowledge of all tongues. Why, therefore, should not the living disciples of Christ do as they did—opening the Scriptures to the people so clearly and plainly, that they may verily understand them, since, except to the unbeliever, disposed to resist the Holy Spirit, the things contained in Scripture are no fiction." Powerfully impressed with the sentiments just quoted, Wycliffe devoted, from about the year 1378, his time and energies to the work of his translation. The time of its completion cannot be fixed, but probably it was the year 1380, or a year or two later.

Wycliffe, not being acquainted with the Hebrew o

Greek languages, made his translations from the Vulgate, the Latin version of the Scriptures. Bagster says, in his Preface to his English Hexapla: "His knowledge of Greek did not extend beyond the few words sprinkled over his writings; and even had he been competent to the task of translating from the original, most likely he could not at that period have found a manuscript for the purpose. In the fourteenth century Greek was almost universally neglected in Western Europe, some traces were found in Italy; but Hallam remarks that on this side of the Alps not one man, except Angerville, is reported to have been versed in Greek during that period."

He adhered most rigidly to the Latin text, which led him into some errors and strange obscurities, making it very unsatisfactory to himself. He contemplated a revision, but was called away by death too soon to complete the work; but it was accomplished by his curate, John Purvey, and it is this revision that is now in use as Wycliffe's Bible. Only one copy of the original version is known to be in existence.

The following comparisons may be of interest to the reader:

WYCLIFFE. ORIGINAL VERSION.

"Therfore whane Jhesus was born in bethleem of Juda in the daies of king eroude loo astronomyens camen fro the eest to Jerusalem and seiden whae is he that is born king of Jewis, for we ban seyn his sterre in the eest and we ban (in the margin, or "ben") camen for to worship im."

WYCLIFFE. REVISED VERSION.

"Therefore when Ihesa was baren in bedlem of juda, in the dayes of kinge heroude, loo kyngis or wise men camen fro the est to ierusalem s yinge where is he that is baren kynge of jews, far-sage we han seen his sterre in the eest and we camen for to worshipe hym."

Throughout the revised version there is no improvement made on Wycliffe's original, but often the reverse.

It is reported that as early as the year 1390 an attempt was made to suppress Wycliffe's translations by act of parliament, but that John of Gaut, Wycliffe's old freind, resisted the iniquitous bill, declaring, "we will not be the dregs of all, seeing other nations have the law of God, which is the law of our faith, written in their own language." Be this, however, as it may, a convocation at Oxford, in the year 1408, enacted a law, commonly called Arundel's Constitution —from the part taken in the measure by the archbishop of that name—by which all unauthorized persons were forbidden to translate any part of the Scripture into English, and every one was warned, under pain of excommunication, against reading any version or treatise, made either in Wycliffe's time, or since, except it should be approved by the diocesan, or a provincial council. Here then was a weapon put into the hands of the enemies of God's Word and the true faith, which they might wield at pleasure against any one found possessing one of the Wycliffe Bibles. The ecclesiastical courts were soon occupied with cases of this description; and from the register of Alnwick, bishop of Norwich, we learn that in 1429, Richard Fletcher, of Beccles, had to appear before his lordship, on the charge of having a book of the new law in English. Nicholas Belward, too, was arraigned for purchasing a New Testament for four marks and forty pence, and teaching William Wright and Margery his wife the study of the same. Others were accused of belonging to the sect of the Lollards, on the ground that they could read English well, and did read in the presence of others the Word of God. As one muses over these old entries in the records of persecution, they bring up vivid illustrations of the state of the times. How revolting to our Christian feelings, that the study of the Scriptures should be alleged against a man in the *spiritual* court as a crime! How wide-spread must have been the ignorance of the people when the ability to read English was enough to attach to a common person a suspicion of heresy. How precious must the Word of God have been in those days, when a Testament was worth $14.00, equal to $224.00 now, taking, on the authority of Mr. Hallam, sixteen as the multiple for bringing down the money of that time to our standard.

CHAPTER III.

TYNDALE AND HIS TRANSLATIONS.

William Tyndale, who is called the patriarch of the Authorized Version, was born in Gloucestershire in 1477 or 1484. The dates given by writers differ. He was educated at Oxford, and "became learned in the knowledge of tongues and liberal acts." About 1520 he became tutor in in the house of Sir John Walsh, at Sodbury Mansion, near Bristol. Here he pursued his sacred studies, and enlarged his acquaintance with revelation, till the sublime thought of translating the Scriptures into the English language became a purpose. But he could not find, while he remained among the Gloucestershire priests, that quietude and liberty which were necessary for the prosecution of his design; and therefore, being "so turmoiled," as he says, he was glad to make his escape, and seek elsewhere a place in which to carry out his fixed resolution. "As I this thought," he tells us, "the bishop of London came to my remembrance, whom Erasmus praiseth exceedingly, among others in his Annotations on the New Testament, for his great learning. Then, thought I, if I might come to this man's service, I were happy. And so I gat me to London, and, through the acquaintance of my master, came to Sir Harry Gilford, the king's grace's comptroller, and brought him an oration of Isocrates, which I had translated out of the Greek into English, and desired him to speak unto my lord of London for me; which he also did as he showed me, and willed me to write an epistle to my lord, and go to him myself, which I also did, and delivered my epistle to a servant of his own, one William Hebilthwayte, a man of mine old acquaintance. But God (which knoweth what is within hypocrites) saw that I was beguiled, and that that counsel was not the next way unto my purpose. And therefore he got me no favor in my lord's sight. Whereupon my lord answered me his house was full, he had more than he could well find, and advised me to seek in London, where he said I could not lack a service. And so in London I abode almost a year, and marked the course of the world, and heard our praters — I would say our preachers — how they boasted themselves and their high authority, and beheld the pomp of our prelates, and how busy they were, as they yet are, to set aside peace and unity in the world, and saw things whereof I defer to speak at this time, and understood at the last not only that there was no room in my lord of London's palace, to translate the New Testament, but also that there was no place to do it in all England, as experience doth now openly declare."

This was written in 1530, and relates to what took place in 1524. Poor Tyndale! In vain he sought the patronage of the metropolitan bishop — no encouragement from that quarter could he find in his heaven-born undertaking. "Room enough," he quaintly remarks, in the margin of the book in which the above quoted observations occur, "room enough there was in my lord's house for belly cheer, but none to translate the New Testament." Indeed, Tyndale had hard work to live at all in London, and would have been in positive destitution but for the friendship of the wealthy citizen and alderman named Humphry Monmouth. Hearing

CHAPTER III.

TYNDALE AND HIS TRANSLATIONS.

William Tyndale, who is called the patriarch of the Authorized Version, was born in Gloucestershire in 1477 or 1484. The dates given by writers differ. He was educated at Oxford, and "became learned in the knowledge of tongues and liberal acts." About 1520 he became tutor in in the house of Sir John Walsh, at Sodbury Mansion, near Bristol. Here he pursued his sacred studies, and enlarged his acquaintance with revelation, till the sublime thought of translating the Scriptures into the English language became a purpose. But he could not find, while he remained among the Gloucestershire priests, that quietude and liberty which were necessary for the prosecution of his design; and therefore, being "so turmoiled," as he says, he was glad to make his escape, and seek elsewhere a place in which to carry out his fixed resolution. "As I this thought," he tells us, "the bishop of London came to my remembrance, whom Erasmus praiseth exceedingly, among others in his Annotations on the New Testament, for his great learning. Then, thought I, if I might come to this man's service, I were happy. And so I gat me to London, and, through the acquaintance of my master, came to Sir Harry Gilford, the king's grace's comptroller, and brought him an oration of Isocrates, which I had translated out of the Greek into English, and desired him to speak unto my lord of London for me; which he also did as he showed me, and willed me to write an epistle to my lord, and go to him myself, which I also did, and delivered my epistle to a servant of his own, one William Hebilthwayte, a man of mine old acquaintance. But God (which knoweth what is within hypocrites) saw that I was beguiled, and that that counsel was not the next way unto my purpose. And therefore he got me no favor in my lord's sight. Whereupon my lord answered me his house was full, he had more than he could well find, and advised me to seek in London, where he said I could not lack a service. And so in London I abode almost a year, and marked the course of the world, and heard our praters — I would say our preachers — how they boasted themselves and their high authority, and beheld the pomp of our prelates, and how busy they were, as they yet are, to set aside peace and unity in the world, and saw things whereof I defer to speak at this time, and understood at the last not only that there was no room in my lord of London's palace, to translate the New Testament, but also that there was no place to do it in all England, as experience doth now openly declare."

This was written in 1530, and relates to what took place in 1524. Poor Tyndale! In vain he sought the patronage of the metropolitan bishop — no encouragement from that quarter could he find in his heaven-born undertaking. "Room enough," he quaintly remarks, in the margin of the book in which the above quoted observations occur, "room enough there was in my lord's house for belly cheer, but none to translate the New Testament." Indeed, Tyndale had hard work to live at all in London, and would have been in positive destitution but for the friendship of the wealthy citizen and alderman named Humphry Monmouth. Hearing

Tyndale preach at St. Dunstan's in the West, he inquired into his circumstances, and finding he had no means of support, and being afterwards requested by Tyndale to render him some assistance, he kindly took him into his house for half a year, "and there," says sir Humphry, "he lived like a good priest as me thought. He studied most part of the day and of the night at his book, and he would eat but sodden meat by his good will, nor drink but small single beer. I never saw him wear linen about him in the space he was with me." Providence was preparing the way for Tyndale to execute the holy task upon which he had set his mind, and which was at once to purify his own religious sentiments, and to prove powerfully instrumental in dispersing much of this papal darkness from off the face of his beloved country. But, as it often happens in this world, the reformer and friend of the church had to perform his high behest amidst persecution and sufferings, and to receive from his fellow-men no other reward than the crown of martyrdom. Bidding adieu to his native shores—an everlasting adieu as it proved in the sequel—Tyndale sailed over to Hamburgh in the year 1524.

In 1525 we find him at Cologne, far advanced in the prosecution of his purpose. The press was at work upon his New Testament. In those times it was necessary, in order to succeed, that such a man should act with silence and secrecy; and, therefore, being unobserved by his contemporaries, and keeping the story of his progress to himself, the remembrance of most of his personal adventures in the execution of his work has perished. Probably, at Hamburgh, he was busily employed with the translation, deriving his support from the generous Monmouth and other Christian merchants, who had begun to embrace the new learning.

But there was one man named Cochlæus, a deacon of the Church of the Blessed Virgin, at Frankfort, who got a glimpse of what Tyndale was doing. "Having become intimate and familiar with the Cologne printers, he sometimes heard them confidently boast, when in their cups, that whether the king and cardinal of England would or not, all England would in a short time be Lutheran. He heard, also, that there were two Englishmen lurking there, skilful in language, and fluent, whom, however, he never could see or converse with. Calling, therefore, certain printers into his lodging, after they were heated with wine, one of them, in more private discourse, revealed to him the secret by which England was to be drawn over to the side of Luther, namely, that three thousand copies of the Lutheran New Testament, translated into the English language, were in the press, and already were advanced as far as the letter K, in printing the forms; that the expenses were wholly supplied by English merchants, who were secretly to convey the work, when printed, and to disperse it widely through all England, before the king or the cardinal could discover or prohibit it.

"Cochlæus being inwardly affected by fear and wonder, disguised his grief, under the appearance of admiration. But another day considering with himself the magnitude of the grievous danger, he cast in mind by what method he might expeditiously obstruct these very wicked attempts. He went, therefore, secretly, to Herman Rinck, a patrician of Cologne, and military knight, familiar both with the emperor and the king of England, and a councillor, and disclosed to him the whole affair, as, by means of the wine, he had received it. He, that he might ascertain all things more certainly, sent another person into the house where the work was printing, according to the discovery of Cochlæus, and when he had understood from him that the matter was even so, and that there was great abundance of paper there, he went to the senate, and so brought it about that the printer was interdicted from proceeding further in that work. The two English apostates, snatching away with them the quarto sheets printed, fled by ship, going up the Rhine to Worms, where the people were under the full rage of Lutheranism, that there, by another printer, they might complete the work begun."

The Testament, interrupted in its progress at Cologne, was in quarto, and it had a prologue, and certain notes. It could easily be identified as Tyndale's, by those, who had discovered what he was doing. At Worms, therefore, he changed his plan. He immediately commenced an octavo edition of the book, without prologue or notes. This he speedily finished, and at once issued it from the press. It was the first New Testament printed in English that ever saw the light. "That the rudeness of the work now at the first time offered, offend them not," are the words of the translator in the postscript to his book. But, though the quarto edition was for a little while left incomplete, Tyndale resumed his labors, and completed it. First in design and partial execution, it was the last in publication.

A precious relic of the old quarto was discovered some years ago, by a Mr. Rodd, containing the prologue and the Gospel of Matthew, as far as the twenty-second chapter. The only perfect copy of the octavo edition, known to be in existence, is preserved in the Baptist College Library, Bristol. One other copy is in existence, but lacks forty-eight leaves.

All preceding versions of the Scriptures in English had been made from the Latin Vulgate, but this was from the Greek original, as an examination of Tyndale's labors abundantly shows; and to the accuracy of his translation a striking proof is afforded by the fact, that though the English New Testament underwent so many revisions before it appeared in its present form, a very considerable portion of Tyndale's version remains in it unaltered.

Stealthily brought over to England, probably by way of Antwerp, or through Holland, the Testaments of Tyndale were soon circulated far and wide. George Herman, a citizen of Antwerp, and Simon Fish, of Gray's Inn, London, appear to have been active agents in the enterprise, and deserve to be ranked among their country's best benefactors.

In October, 1526, the bishop of London published a prohibition of Tyndale's Testament. Diligent search was made by the alarmed priests of Rome for the new translation. Those who were detected with it in their possession were treated as heretics; and the fate of the proscribed books was to be cast into the fire. But fresh importations soon supplied the loss. After the quarto edition was completed at Worms, a printer at Antwerp set his press to work upon the book, and issued a third edition in 1526. This was succeeded in the next year by a fourth, printed in the same city. The merchants of the Steelyard, about that time, were lading their ships with wheat from the continental ports to meet a great scarcity which then prevailed in London:

on board these same vessels there came spiritual stores, copies of the word of life—the bread from heaven. As many as four or five hundred Testaments were imported by one man.

What was to be done? As early as 1527, it was suggested that the books should be bought up as fast as they could be obtained, and burned. Archbishop Warham entered into the scheme, and spent 56£ 11s. 4d. about $280.00, equal in our time to at least $4000.00, upon it. To assist in covering the expense, he wrote to the bishops for subscriptions, and a letter is preserved, written by poor old Nix, bishop of Norwich, at the time quite blind, who contributed ten marks to the object, and most fervently pronounced the archbishop's undertaking "a gracious and blessed deed." Tonstall, bishop of London, improved on his grace's idea, and sought to destroy the Testaments by wholesale. His plan was to buy up copies at Antwerp, where they were printed. He happened to be in that city in 1529, and there he employed a man, named Packington, to make the bargain, and get the books.

There was a great gathering in the churchyard of old St. Paul's, on the 4th of May, 1530. The spectacle-loving folks of those days might be seen wending up Ludgate Hill, and along the side of Cheape, to assemble round St. Paul's Cross. The promenade in the middle aisle of the old Gothic cathedral — where London citizens were wont to saunter and chat, transact business and while away an idle hour — was almost emptied by the attractive influence of the scene to be enacted without the walls. The English Bibles, which had been purchased, were to be burned. Tonstall caused the books he had obtained at Antwerp to be committed to the flames. Testament after Testament was flung on the blazing pyre—the people were solemnly warned against the sin of reading the word of God! The church, she was the only teacher! The Bible was not for the people to read, but for the priest to explain! The version made in the English tongue by a thoughtful, learned, pious mind, was only fit for the flames! The crowds about the old churchyard looked on the spectacle that day with varied feelings. Some thought all this was right; others, that it was all wrong. "This burning," says Burnet, "had such a hateful appearance in it, being generally called a burning of the Word of God, that people from thence concluded there must be a visible contrariety between that book and the doctrines of those who handled it; by which both their prejudice against the clergy, and their desire of reading the New Testament was increased."

But, in spite of searchings and burnings, proclamations, and buying up of editions, the hated Testaments still found their way from the continent: sometimes inclosed in packages, artfully covered with flax, and sometimes conveyed among the ware of Jewish merchants. "Sir," said the bishop of London to his agent, Packington, "how cometh this, that there are so many New Testaments abroad, and you promised and assured me you had bought all?"—"I promised you," rejoined Packington, "I bought all that then was to be had; but I perceive they have made more since, and it will never be better as long as they have the letters and stamps; therefore it were best for your lordship to buy the stamps too, and then you are sure." The bishop smiled at him, and said, "Well, Packington, well;" and so ended the matter. "And so perhaps," adds Mr.

Anderson, "ended the device of purchasing books in order to burn them, but it will not be long before we find these enemies to proceed to the men themselves, and with a bitter zeal, still more inflamed, consign them to the fire; for very soon after this, seizing and burning men, instead of their productions or the books in their possession, became the order of the day."

In 1530 Tyndale published his translation of the Pentateuch, which was the commencement of his labors on the Old Testament; labors which he prosecuted to a great extent, though he did not finish the sacred volume, and for which he was qualified by his acquaintance with the Hebrew, as well as the Greek and Latin tongues. In the following year, he printed his version of Jonah; and in 1534, he issued a revised translation of the New Testament. In this work he sought to render the English more idiomatic, and was not above availing himself of any hints to be derived from hostile criticisms on the edition of 1526.

A man like Tyndale, so incessantly and quietly plying his pen in the translation of the Scriptures, and the vindication of Scripture truths, was not likely to be unmolested by the church at Rome, and by the enemies of a free circulation of the Bible. Henry VIII., though he had broken with Rome, and had commenced the course which, by the controlling providence of God, proved subservient to the cause of reformation, was an inveterate enemy to the use of Tyndale's version, and published a proclamation against it, for which, no doubt, he was the more ready, because Tyndale had condemned the divorce of Catherine. But how much more effectual a thing to get the man himself into his hands! Measures were, therefore, employed to decoy him over to England. Sir Stephen Vaughan, Henry's agent in the Netherlands, did his utmost to persuade him to return. But Tyndale, though ready to die in defence of truth, did not see it to be his duty to thrust his head into the lion's mouth, and, therefore, very wisely preferred to remain on the continent.

Tyndale was betrayed into the hands of his enemies by an unprincipled Englishman, named Philips. This man had professed friendship for the noble-hearted reformer, and had, on the very morning of the betrayal, borrowed of him forty shillings. Under the guidance of this second Iscariot, the officers proceeded to Tyndale's place of abode, when Philips entered, and bringing out his unsuspecting victim, "gave the men a sign," who immediately seized upon their prey, and conveyed him to the castle of Vilvord, near Brussels. The unresisting meekness, the transparent simplicity of the good man affected the very officers ; and during his captivity his pious conversation was made useful to the gaoler and his family. He lingered between one and two years in prison, and employed his time partly in controversy with the priests of Louvain, and partly in preparing a translation of the New Testament, with a provincial orthography suited to rustic laborers ; thus redeeming to the letter his early pledge to give the plough-boy the Word of God.

In September, 1536, he was led forth to execution, and having been first strangled, his body was thrown into the flames. His last breath went up to heaven in the well-known prayer: "Lord, open the eyes of the king of England !" At whose instigation was Tyndale thus barbarously sacrificed ? Much of obscurity rests on the transaction, but there can be little doubt that the enemies of the reformer in England were the promptcrs of the deed ; and Mr. Anderson has adduced evidence to show that both Cromwell and Cranmer were aware of Tyndale's position, but declined to make any attempt for his deliverance. It seemed the destiny of this extraordinary man, through life, to be unpatronized by the mighty ones of this world.

CHAPTER IV.

COVERDALE AND HIS TRANSLATIONS

Coverdale, the friend of Cromwell, Earl of Essex, was born in Yorkshire, 1488. He was educated at Cambridge, in the home of the Augustine friars, and after having been admitted into that order, was ordained priest at Norwich in 1514. On the promulgation of the Reformed opinions at Cambridge, Coverdale was among the first to abandon his allegiance to the church of Rome; and probably finding it unsafe to remain in England, he went abroad, and, according to Foxe, assisted Tyndale in translating the Bible.

Coverdale remained in obscurity until 1535, when he published his own translation, with a dedication to Henry VIII, who had now come to an irreparable breach with the Pope. In his translation he followed closely his friend Tyndale in the Old Testament, and the Zurich translation for the rest of the books of the Old Testament which Tyndale did not translate. And in the New Testament, completed in 1538, where he varied from Tyndale, he followed either the Zurich version, Sanctus Pagnimos, Luther, or the Vulgate. In the Preface he says: "Considering how excellent knowledge and learning an interpreter of Scripture ought to have in the tongues, and pondering also mine own insufficiency therein, and how weak I am to perform the office of a translator, I was the more loath to meddle with this work. Notwithstanding, when I considered how great pity it was that we should want it so long, and called to my remembrance the adversity of them who were not only of ripe knowledge, but would also, with all their hearts, have performed that they begun, if they had not had impediment" (here, no doubt, he alludes to Tyndale, then in prison), "considering, I say, that, by reason of their adversity, it could not so soon have been brought to an end as our most prosperous nation would fain have had it — these and other reasonable causes considered, I was the more bold to take it in hand."

Wanly supposes that it was in Zurich that Coverdale printed his Bible, and we love to think of that cheerful city, " embosomed among vine-clad knolls, meadows, and orchards, and surmounted by forests, above and beyond which appear the loftier summits of the Alps, with our English translator working in some little room, through the live-long day, till long after the sun had set behind those Alpine heights, then rising to his task again, before the same sun gilded the opposite horizon. On and on he labored, till the colophon at the end of the last sheet proclaimed that the top stone of his work was laid — with what joy may be better conceived than told! No time would be lost in packing up the sheets, in conveying them to the nearest and most convenient port, and in shipping them for England. While the early winds of that Winter were sweeping the German Ocean, a bark might be seen buffeted by the waters, but watched over by the eye and guarded by the hand of God, containing, among meaner freightage, a cargo of English Bibles, translated by Miles Coverdale—a treasure more precious far than the golden fleece brought by the Argonauts of old from the land of Colchis."

The book was well received in England. Cromwell patronized it. The dedication to Henry VIII. was in keeping with the custom of the age in such matters, and indicates that the translator hoped for the royal smile. The story related by Coverdale, in a sermon at St. Paul's Cross, indicates that in this respect he was not altogether disappointed. "After it was finished, and presented to King Henry VIII., and by him committed to several bishops of that time to peruse, of which I remember Stephen Gardiner was one, after they had kept it long in their hands, and the king was divers times sued unto for the publication thereof, at the last being called for by the king himself, they redelivered the book, and being demanded by the king what they thought of the translation, they answered that there were many faults therein. 'Well,' said the king, 'but are there any heresies maintained thereby?' They answered, 'that there were no heresies that they could find.' 'If there be no heresies,' said the king, 'then, in God's name, let it go abroad among the people.'"

This was the first translation of the entire Bible published in the English language, and the Psalms of it are now used in the Book of Common Prayer. With the sanction of the king, Coverdale went to Paris in 1538 to superintend the publication of a new edition; but a decree of the Inquisition broke up the printing-establishment, and consigned the sheets already finished to the flames. A few copies, however, having been sold as waste paper, were preserved; and there, with the presses which were transported to England, were used, under the superintendence of Coverdale, in printing the "Great Bible" of Cranmer. A copy was presented to Lord Cromwell, asking his intercession for the royal authority. A royal proclamation informed people that it had pleased the king to permit and command that the Bible, printed in the English language, should be used for instruction in every parish.

The Roman party greatly opposed the printing of the Bible in English, and especially its free distribution and use by the people, but the friends of the Reformation were encouraged, and the people all over England attended in crowds to hear the book read.

CHAPTER V.

MATTHEW'S BIBLE AND THE GREAT BIBLE.

According to Strype, in his Life of Cranmer, the archbishop, in the same year in which Coverdale prepared his version (1535), made an attempt to get one executed in England by the bishops. "He began with the translation of the New Testament: taking an old English translation thereof (either Tyndale's or Wycliffe's), which he divided into nine or ten parts, causing each part to be written at large in a paper book, and then to be sent to the best learned bishops and others to the intent that they should make a perfect correction thereof. And when they had done, he required them to send back their parts, so corrected, unto him at Lambeth, by a day limited for that purpose: and the same course, no question, he took with the Old Testament. It chanced that the Acts of the Apostles was sent to Bishop Stokesley to oversee and correct. When the day came, every man had sent to Lambeth their parts corrected, only Stokesley's portion was wanting. My lord of Canterbury wrote to the bishop a letter for his part, requiring him to deliver them unto the bringer, his secretary. He received the archbishop's letter at Fulham, unto which he made this answer: 'I marvel what my lord of Canterbury meaneth, that thus abuseth the people in giving them liberty to read the Scriptures, which doth nothing else but infect them with heresy. I have bestowed never an hour on my portion, nor never will, and therefore my lord shall have this book again: for I will never be guilty of leading the simple people into error.' My lord of Canterbury's servant took the book and brought the same to Lambeth unto my lord, declaring my lord of London's answer. When the archbishop had perceived that the bishop had done nothing therein, 'I marvel,' said he, 'that my lord of London is so froward that he will not do as other men do.' One Mr. Thomas Launey stood by, and hearing my lord speak so much of the bishop's untowardness, said, 'I can tell your grace why my lord of London will not bestow any labor or pains this way. Your grace knoweth well that his portion is a piece of the New Testament. But he being persuaded that Christ had bequeathed him nothing in his Testament, thought it mere madness to bestow any labor or pain where no gain was to be gotten. And besides this, it is the Acts of the Apostles, which were simple poor fellows, and therefore my lord of London disdained to have to do with any of them.' Whereat my lord of Canterbury, and others who stood by, could not forbear from laughter." For the present, all attempts at executing a translation of a Bible in England failed; still we must turn to the continent in order to witness the progress of efforts of this kind; there we are to discover the chosen instruments of God's favor to the English church, among humble and obscure strangers in a foreign land. John Rogers had been chaplain to an English congregation at Antwerp, and had become acquainted with Tyndale during his residence in that city. Before his acquaintance with that illustrious exile, he had been a zealous Papist, but, by his intercourse with him at Antwerp, he was led to see into the errors of Popery, and to adopt the views of the reformer. Having been educated at Cambridge, and possessing the reputation of "a very able linguist and general scholar," he was fitted by Providence to follow Tyndale in his particular path of usefulness as a Biblical translator; and, accordingly, after Tyndale's death, he set to work to complete the version of the Old Testament which Tyndale had begun. Foxe states that a packet of papers was sent by the martyr, on the morning of his execution, to his faithful friend Poyntz; and it has been supposed that they contained the unpublished part of Tyndale's version as far as he had proceeded with it. Perhaps it was from Poyntz that this came into the hands of Rogers, whereupon he devoted himself to the publication of the manuscript. "The object that Rogers had in view was to forward the work and do justice to the labors of the man he admired. Accordingly, the whole of the New Testament, and of the Old, as far as the end of the second of Chronicles, or exactly two-thirds of the entire Scriptures, are Tyndale's, verbally, with an occasional variation only in the orthography; and as for the other third, while Rogers may have taken advantage of Coverdale's printed sheets, he evidently had sat in judgment on every page, and his method is not implicitly followed. Rogers had the whole of Tyndale's, whether in print or manuscript, as well as Coverdale's sheets for the remainder, before him; and having now arrived at the close we find these words: "To the honoure and prayse of God was this Byble prynted, and fynesshed in the yere of oure Lorde God, MDXXXVII." At the end of the Old Testament, the letters W. T., evidently intended for William Tyndale, are conspicuously inserted, and adorned with flourishes, as an acknowledgment of the large share which his labors had contributed to the volume. The exhortation to the study of the Bible, prefixed to the book, is signed J. R., the initials of Rogers, thus pointing him out as the editor. The work was commonly ascribed to this excellent man at the time, although the name given to it was that of Matthew's Bible, Thomas Matthew being a fictitious name assumed by Rogers for the occasion, when concealment, in such matters, was sought for the sake of personal safety. Rogers, now distinguished for his labors, was afterwards distinguished for his sufferings. He was the first martyr who suffered in Smithfield in Queen Mary's days, and led all the rest.

Grafton and Whitchurch, two famous printers at that time, executed the work on the continent — where, cannot be determined. As soon as it was complete, they forwarded it to Cranmer, who expressed his delightful surprise at the sight of the volume, and forwarded it to Cromwell. "I understand," says the archbishop — afterwards, in a letter to the powerful minister of state — "that your lordship, at my request, hath not only exhibited the Bible which I sent unto you to the king's majesty, but also hath obtained of his grace that the same shall be allowed, by his authority, to be bought and read within this realm." Probably, Cromwell's influence with Henry at that time had much to do with the obtaining of the royal sanction of the work: at any rate, on the title-page of the Bible appear the much-coveted words: "Set forth with the king's most gracyous licence." And thus Henry unwittingly afforded his public sanction to the man whom he had persecuted through life, and whom he had permitted to die a felon's death on a foreign shore!

The king's license being granted for this book, and the chains being thus far taken off the press, Matthew's Bible was speedily reprinted by Nicholson, a printer in Southwark. The book became the favorite one and superseded the version of Coverdale. But still Coverdale continued his Biblical labors, and, in 1538, published "a new version of the New Testament," and also an edition of the English Testament, together with the text of the Latin Vulgate. He also paraphrased some of the Psalms, with more of pious zeal than poetic taste.

In the same year, 1539, another edition appeared, edited by Richard Taverner, who dedicates the volume to the king, and remarks, that his grace never did anything more acceptable to God than the act of licensing the most sacred Bible, containing the "unspotted and hoily Word of God." It is a mere revision of Matthew's Bible which Taverner published; and he informs us, in his preface, that as the printers were desirous to have the Bible come forth as faultless as the shortness of the time for the recognizing of the same would permit, they desired him to overlook and peruse the whole copy, and amend the same according to the true examplers, which, according to his talent, he had gladly done. "This Taverner was a strange genius. He was of the Inner Temple, where he loved to display his pedantry, by citing the law in Greek. In the reign of Edward, he became a preacher by royal license, and sometimes appeared in the pulpit dressed in a damask gown, velvet bonnet, and gold chain, in which uncanonical attire he delivered a discourse before the youthful sovereign!" In the reign of Elizabeth, he resumed his pulpit exercises, and when high sheriff of Oxfordshire he held forth before the university, wearing, in addition to his other unclerical dress, a sword by his side. "Surely," says Fuller, "preaching now ran very low, if it be true what I read, that Mr. Taverner, of Water Eaton, in Oxfordshire, high sheriff of the county, gave the scholars a sermon in St. Mary's, with his gold chain about his neck, and his sword by his side, beginning with these words : 'Arriving at the Mount of St. Mary's, in the stony stage where I now stand, I have brought you some fine biscuits, baked in the oven of charity, and carefully conserved for the chickens of the church, the sparrows of the spirit, and the sweet swallows of salvation!'"

The Great Bible now claims our attention. The introduction and notes in Matthew's Bible, and the faulty translation, rendered it objectional to the clergy, particularly because of the heresy these notes were supposed to teach; hence they often petitioned the king that a new version might be printed. It was not, however, until Cromwell came into power that such a work was commenced, and it was doubtless under his influence and direction that the work was begun. He himself was a great lover of the Scriptures, and it is said he could repeat the entire Latin version of the New Testament made by Erasmus. He appointed Grafton as printer, Coverdale as editor, and Paris as the place where it should be printed, because the better paper and better workmen could be obtained than in England. The work was begun in 1538, but was soon interrupted by the Inquisitor-general; but Coverdale and Grafton, with the workmen, types, and presses, escaped to London, where the work was completed in 1539. It was a revision of Matthew's Bible; but Coverdale followed to some extent, in the Old Testament, Munster's Latin version, and Erasmus' Latin version in the New Testament. This is sometimes called Whitchurch's Bible, but he was only one of the printers of the first edition. It was called "the Great Bible," because of its size, it being over fifteen inches long and nine inches wide, an unusual size in those times.

Cranmer's Bible was published in 1540 by the direction of Archbishop Cranmer, who wrote the prologue, although Coverdale was the editor. While this is a revision of the Great Bible, it differs in many places widely from it. How much personal work was done by Cranmer is not known, but of his ability there can be no question, as he was one of the finest classical scholars of his day. Tonstal, bishop of Durham, and Heath, bishop of Rochester, assisted him. A revised edition was published in 1541, and this was the authorized version for twenty-seven years, except during the regin of Queen Mary.

CHAPTER VI.

THE GENEVAN BIBLE.

William Whittingham was born in 1524, in Lanchester, near Durham. He was educated in Oxford, and afterward spent many years in foreign travel. He returned home to England in 1553, but soon left again for the continent. In 1554 he was pastor of an English church in Frankfort. In 1555 he married Catherine Jaquemayne, of Orleans, the sister of John Calvin's wife. In 1556 he became successor of John Knox as pastor of the English exiles in Geneva. Here he translated the New Testament, which appeared in 1557. An eloquent preface to it was written by John Calvin.

The Genevan Testament was a much more original work than any other translation since Tyndale's. The translator availed himself of the labors of his predecessors, and often followed the version in the Great Bible; but he evidently studied the original for himself, and exercised an independent judgment in the choice of his renderings. Notes are introduced in the margin of the Testament, and for the first time we find the English Scriptures divided into verses, and italics introduced to denote those words which have no corresponding ones in the original. It may be added, that the book is a very beautiful specimen of typography in silver type, and on the best paper.

It was issued from the press while the fires were blazing in Smithfield, and found its way to England not long afterwards.

It had this title:

The |Newe Testa-|ment of our Lord Ie-|sus Christ. |Conferred dilligently with the Greke, and best approved translations, |with the arguments, aswel before the chapters, as for every Boke| & Epistle, also diversities of readings, and moste proffitable | annotations of all harde places : whereunto is added a copi-|ous Table. At *Geneva*|Printed By Conrad Badius|M. D. LVII.|

Some time after Whittingham had completed the Genevan Testament, he set to work, in connexion with others, upon the preparation of the Genevan Bible. This, as we learn from their own statement, occupied them "two years and more, day and night." As it was completed in April, 1560, it must have been commenced in the year 1558. The version in the New Testament of this last edition does not exactly agree with that published in 1557, but is plainly a revision of it; and the Old Testament has a much better claim to be regarded as a new translation than any other since Coverdale's. The men who prepared it were scholars, acquainted with the original; and, though they derived assistance from other versions, did not follow any of them with servility.

Whittingham's associates in the work were, probably, Thomas Sampson and Anthony Gilby. Sampson was an Oxford man, and had studied in one of the inns of the Court. He went to Strasburg on Mary's accession; but strongly sympathizing with the Puritan party, he went over to Geneva, and united himself to the congregation there. Gilby was a Cambridge man, and fled to the continent at the commencement of Mary's reign. He was prominent in the Frankfort disputes, which led to his removal to Geneva. Both these divines were distinguished by their learning, and their ardent zeal for the reformed faith.

Miles Coverdale, Thomas Cole, Christopher Goodmen, John Knox, John Pullain and John Bodleigh are thought to have assisted in the work, but some of them could have done very little work on it. Whittingham, Sampson and Gilby did the greater part of the work of translating.

This was the first English Bible printed in Roman type and the first broken up into verses. It was a small 4to with the following title:

The Bible | and Holy Scriptures | Conteyned in | the Olde and Newe | Testament, | Translated According to the Ebrue and Greke, and conferred With | the best translations in divers languages. | With moste profitable Annota- | tions upon all the hard places, and other things of great | importance as may appeare in the Epistle to the Reader. | *At Geneva,* | Printed by Rowland Hall. | M. D. LX.

The following is a sample of this book, from 1 Cor. xv. 29–32.

29. Els what shal they do which are baptized for dead? if the dead rise not at all, why are they then baptized for dead?

30. Why are we also in ieoperdie everie houre?

32. If I have foght with beastes at Ephesus after the maner of men, what avantageth it me, if the dead be not raised up? let us eat & drinke: for to marowe we shall dye.

CHAPTER VII.

THE BISHOP'S BIBLE.

The two principal Bibles in use during the early part of the reign of Queen Elizabeth were the Great Bible and the Genevan. Neither of these were satisfactory to Archbishop Parker, who made preparation for a new translation. We are informed by Strype that Parker "took on himself the labor to contrive, and set the whole work a-going, in a proper method, by sorting out the whole Bible into parcels, and distributing those parcels to able bishops and other learned men, to peruse and collate each of the book or books allotted them; sending, withal, his instructions for the order they should observe; and they were to add some short marginal notes, for the illustration or correction of the text: and all these portions being finished, and sent back to the archbishop, he was to add the last hand to them, and so to take care for printing and publishing the whole." When the bishops had completed their task, they sent back their portions of the version to the archbishop, and certain learned divines in his household re-perused and examined the whole work.

The parties who assisted Archbishop Parker in the preparation of this volume are indicated by their initials being subscribed to the portions executed by them respectively.

W. E., at the end of the Pentateuch, means William Exoniensis, or William Allen, bishop of Exeter, who succeeded Coverdale. He was an Oxford man of great learning.

R. M., at the close of the second book of Samuel, was Richardus Menevensis, or Richard Davies, bishop of St. David's, an exile in the reign of Mary, and afterwards bishop of St. Asaph, when he was translated to St. David's.

E. W., at the end of the second of Chronicles, Edwin Wigornensis, were the initials of the famous Edwin Sandys, bishop of Worcester. He was vice-chancellor of Cambridge at the time of Edward the Sixth's death, and supported the title of poor lady Jane Grey to the crown. For this he was stripped of all but his Bible, and was confined in prison in company with the noble-hearted John Bradford.

A. P. C., at the conclusion of Job, was Andrew Peerson, prebendary of Canterbury, an esteemed friend of Parker, to whom he was chaplain and almoner.

T. B., at the end of the Psalms, refers to Thomas Becon, the well-known author of many valued publications. This portion of the book was originally allotted to Guest, who returned it to the archbishop after making some slight alterations in the version taken from the Great Bible.

A. P. C., at the end of Proverbs, mean Andrew Peerson, prebendary of Canterbury.

A. P. E., at the close of Canticles, indicate Andrew Perne, prebend of Ely.

R. W., at the conclusion of the Lamentations, stands for Robert Horne, bishop of Winchester, an exile in Mary's reign, and a zealous Protestant.

T. C. L., at the end of Daniel, evidently denote Thomas Bentham, bishop of Lichfield and Coventry.

He was a man of distinguished learning, but still more eminent for his deep piety.

E. L., are the initials of Edmund Grindale, bishop of London, chaplain to Ridley, an exile under Mary, bishop of London after her death, and finally, archbishop of York.

J. N., appear at the end of the Apocrypha, meaning John Parkhurst, bishop of Norwich, a pious and learned divine, and very moderate in his views of the ecclesiastical questions of the day.

R. E., at the end of Acts, point to Richard Cox, bishop of Ely. He had been early persecuted for circulating Tyndale's Testament, and in Mary's reign rendered himself notorious by the part he took in the troubles of Frankfort.

G. G., are written at the end of the first Epistle to the Corinthians, meaning Gabriel Goodman, dean of Westminster. No other initials appear, and it cannot be determined who prepared the remainder.

It took three or four years to complete this work, when a copy was presented to the queen on October 5, 1568.

It contained one hundred and forty-three engravings, including maps and portraits. The system of verses in the Genevan Bible was followed, but with this was united the old system of alphabetical divisions in the margin.

This Bible never received the Royal sanction, and it was not until two years after Parker's death that an edition was printed "set forth by authoritie," and then this authority was simply episcopal, and not royal. In 1571 it was ordered by Convocations, that a copy should be placed in every cathedral, and, as far as pos-

4

sible, in every church. Every bishop was also directed to have a copy in the hall or dining-room of his house, so as to be accessible to servants and strangers. With all this it never became popular. For many years it was read in public service, but never replaced the Genevan Bible for family use. The last edition was issued in 1606, while the Genevan continued to be published for many years later.

We give a verse from Mark xiv. 3.

3. And when he was at Bethanie, in the house of Simon the leper, even as he sate at meate, there came a woman havyng an alabaster boxe of very precious oyntment, [called] Narde pistike, and she broke the boxe and poured it on his head.

CHAPTER VIII.

THE RHEIMS AND DOUAY VERSION.

The English Roman Catholics established a seminary at Douay, for the education of young Englishmen for the priesthood, that they might do missionary work in their own country. In 1578, ten years later, this seminary was removed to Rheims, but returned to Douay in 1593. The founder of this seminary was William Allen, who was made cardinal in 1587 and archbishop in 1588. One of the professors in the seminary was the distinguished Hebrew and Greek scholar, Gregory Martin, who had been educated at St. John's College, Oxford. While engaged as instructor in this seminary Martin translated the Bible into English from the Vulgate; he was assisted by Dr. Allen, Dr. Reynolds, Dr. Bristow, and Dr. Worthington.

This version was prepared to counteract the influence of the Genevan version. In the preface the translators say that they have done their work, not because they believe, " 1 of necessitie, that the holy Scriptures should alvaies be in our mother tongue, or 2 that they ought, or were ordained of God, to be read indifferently of all, or 3 could be easily understood of every one that readeth or heareth them in a knowen language."

And again in the preface they admit that their version is for a special purpose, forced upon them by "the present time, state and condition of our countrie, unto which, divers things are either necessarie, or profitable, or medicianable now, that otherwise in the peace of the

Church were neither much requisite, nor perchance wholy tolerable, ... divers heretical translations of the Scriptures, poisoning the people under color of divine authoritie."

The New Testament was a 4to volume published at Rheims in 1582. The Old Testament was published at Douay in two volumes, 4to, in the year 1609, thirty years after its translation; the delay was caused by want of funds to publish it. The whole work was reprinted at Rouen in 1635, and then not again for one hundred and fifteen years, when Dr. Challoner, in 1750, published in London a revised edition in four actavo volumes.

As an illustration of the style of this version we select 1 Cor. xv. 29-33.

29. Otherwise what shal they do that are baptized for the dead, if the dead rise not again at al?

30. Why also are they baptized for them? why also are we in danger every houre?

32. If (according to man) I fought with beasts at Ephesus, what doth it profit me, if the dead rise not againe?

33. *Let us eate and drinke, for to morrow we shal die.*

CHAPTER IX.

THE AUTHORIZED VERSION.

On the 24th of October, James I., who had recently ascended the throne, appointed a meeting to be held for the learning and the determining "things pretended to be amiss in the church." The meeting arose out of the complaints of the Puritans, who early saluted their new sovereign with a list of ecclesiastical grievances, which they besought him to remove. The time fixed for this important conference was the 14th of January, 1604, and the place appointed for holding it was Hampton Court.

On Monday, the 16th of January — the only day of the conference which concerns us in the present work — there might be seen assembling in the withdrawing room of the palace in the presence of the king, who had considerable taste for theological debates, certain prelates of the English church, and a few of the Puritan party, with the well-known Dr. Reynolds at their head. Reynolds objected to certain renderings in the extant versions, and he proposed to his king that there should be a new translation. Bancroft, the bishop of London, who was no friend to the Puritans, did not favor Reynolds' proposition. He remarked, "that if every man's humor should be followed, there would be no end of translating." But James, in this one instance, sided with the Puritans, and professed himself friendly to a new translation. He objected to any notes being appended, and Reynolds concurred with him in this view, for his proposition was to the following effect: "that a translation be made of the whole Bible, as consonant as can be to the original Hebrew and Greek, and this to be set out and printed without any marginal notes, and only to be used in all churches of England in time of Divine service."

On the 22nd of July, the same year, the king wrote to Bancroft. "He stated that he had appointed fifty-four learned men for the translating of the Bible, divers of whom had no ecclesiastical preferment, and the main object of the letter is to enjoin upon Bancroft and the bishops that, whenever a living of twenty pounds per annum was vacant, they should inform his majesty of it, that he might commend to the patron one of the said translators, as a fitting person to hold it, as his reward for his service in the translation. He further required that the bishops should inform themselves of such learned men in their dioceses, and charged them to assist in the work by sending their observations to Mr. Lively, Dr. Harding, or Dr. Andrews." In compliance with the king's command, Bancroft wrote to the bishops, and here ended all the trouble — so far as history records — that James I. ever took respecting the translation which bears his name.

The earl of Salisbury, chancellor of the university of Cambridge, wrote to the vice-chancellor and heads of houses, also conveying to them the expression of the king's pleasure that they should join in the undertaking, by recommending fit persons to assist, and by entertaining the translators at the colleges without any charge, only the poor colleges were to look to the bishop of London to defray any expenses in which they might be involved. The king was very careful to shift all the expenses on others. The money expended in the translation was chiefly supplied by Robert Barker, the printer, who paid 3,500 pounds sterling, or about $17,000.

On the 31st of July, Bancroft sent a copy of the king's letter to Cambridge for the persons who had been selected by the university, as translators, expressing his majesty's approbation of the choice, and his desire that they should meet as early as possible. The following instructions accompanied the letters:

" 1. The ordinary Bible read in the church, commonly called the Bishop's Bible, to be followed, and as little altered as the original will permit.

" 2. The names of the prophets and the holy writers, with the other names in the text, to be retained, as near as may be, accordingly as they are vulgarly used.

" 3. The old ecclesiastical words to be kept, as the word 'church,' not to be translated congregation.

" 4. When any word hath divers significations, that to be kept which hath been most commonly used by the most eminent fathers, being agreeable to the propriety of the place, and the analogie of faith.

" 5. The division of the chapters to be altered, either not at all, or as little as may be, if necessity so require.

" 6. No marginal notes at all to be affixed, but only for the explanation of the Hebrew or Greek words, which cannot, without some circumlocution, so briefly and fitly be expressed in the text.

" 7. Such quotations of places to be marginally set down, as shall serve for the fit references of one Scripture to another.

" 8. Every particular man of each company to take the same chapter or chapters ; and, having translated or amended them severally, by himself, where he thinks good, all to meet together, to confer what they have done, and agree for their part what shall stand.

" 9. As any one company hath dispatched any one

book in this manner, they shall send it to the rest, to be considered of seriously and judiciously; for his majesty is very careful in this point.

"10. If any company, upon the review of the book so sent, shall doubt or differ upon any places, to send them word thereof, to note the places, and therewithal to send their reasons; to which, if they consent not, the difference to be compounded at the general meeting, which is to be of the chief persons of each company, at the end of the work.

"11. When any place of special obscurity is doubted of, letters to be directed, by authority, to send to any learned in the land for his judgment in such a place.

"12. Letters to be sent from every bishop to the rest of his clergie, admonishing them of this translation in hand, and to move and charge as many as, being skilful in the tongues, have taken pains in that kind, to send their particular observations to the company, either at Westminster, Cambridge, or Oxford, according as it was directed before in the king's letter to the archbishop.

"13. The directors in each company to be the deanes of Westminster and Chester for Westminster, and the king's professors in Hebrew and Greek in the two universities.

"These translations to be used when they agree better with the text than the Bishops' Bible. Tyndale's, Coverdale's, Matthew's, Whitchurch's, Geneva."

The list of the individuals to whom the preparation of the new version was entrusted has been carefully preserved and often published. It includes the names of some of the most distinguished divines of the day The translators were divided into six companies; the first company met at Westminster, and to them was committed the Pentateuch, with other historical books, as far as the Second Book of Kings. Dr. Launcelot Andrews, Dean of Westminster, presided. Fuller says of him: "The world wanted learning to know how learned this man was, so skilled in all languages, that some conceive he might, if then living, almost have served as an interpreter-general at the confusion of tongues." He was born 1555, died 1626.

The rest of this company were: Dr. John Overall, Dr. Andrian de Saravia, Dr. Richard Clark, Dr. John Layfield, Dr. Teigh, Mr. Burgley, Mr. Geoffry King, Mr. Richard Thomsen, and Mr. William Bednell.

The second company, consisting of eight persons, met at Cambridge, and they prepared the translation from the beginning of Chronicles to the end of Song of Solomon. Edward Lively, regius professor at Cambridge, and a man of great attainments, presided over this department; he died in 1605, having been professor of Hebrew for twenty-five years; with him were associated John Richardson, fellow of Emanuel; Dr. Laurence Chaderton, a man well skilled in Rabbinical literature; Thomas Harrison, vice-master of Trinity; Roger Andrews, brother to the bishop; Robert Spalding, fellow of St. John's, and Lively's successor in the Hebrew chair; and Dr. Andrew Byng, who subsequently occupied the same professorship.

The third company assembled at Oxford, and consisted of seven members, who undertook the rest of the Old Testament from Isaiah to Malachi. Dr. John Harding, regius professor of Hebrew, was chosen to preside over this party, which consisted besides of Dr. John Reynolds, the Puritan, who suggested the new version; Dr. Thomas Holland, a very Apollos, "mighty in the Scriptures;" Dr. Richard Kilbie, a great Hebraist; Dr. Miles Smith, "who had Hebrew at his fingers' ends," says Anthony Wood; Dr. Brett, a good Grecian and orientalist, and Mr. Fairelough.

The fourth company was convened at Oxford, consisting of eight members, who received for their portion of labor the four Gospels, the Acts of the Apostles, and the Revelation of John. Dr. Ravis, dean of Christ Church, was president; the famous George Abbott, dean of Winchester, and afterwards archbishop of Canterbury; Dr. Eedes, dean of Worcester; Dr. Giles Tomson, dean of Windsor; sir Henry Saville, provost of Eton; Dr. Perrin, Greek professor; Dr. Ravens; and Mr. John Harman, were the members of this division.

The fifth company met at Westminster, and translated the Epistles. It consisted of Dr. Barlowe, dean of Chester, afterwards successively bishop of Rochester and Lincoln; Dr. Hutchinson; Dr. Spencer; Mr. Fenton; Mr. Rabbett; Mr. Sanderson, and Mr. Dakins.

The sixth company held their sittings at Cambridge, and undertook the translation of the Apocrypha. They were as follows: Dr. John Duport, prebendary of Ely; Dr. Branthwaite, fellow of Emanuel; Dr. Jeremiah Radcliffe, fellow of Trinity; Dr. Samuel Ward, of Emanuel; Andrew Downes, Greek professor; the celebrated Mr. Bois; and Mr. Ward, fellow of King's.

This great work was not strictly a translation, but a revision of all the English Bibles. It is hard to tell what Hebrew text the revisers used, most likely Bomberg's Rabbinical Bible. In the New Testament they depended mainly upon Beza's Greek Testament, fourth edition, 1589. Besides this they had the Polyglot edition of Erasmus, and the Greek Testament of Stephens. They also made use of the Rhemish version, and of the Spanish, French, Italian, and German translations. A writer says: "They met together, and one read the translation, the rest holding in their hands some Bible, either of the learned tongues, or French, Spanish, Italian, etc. If they found any fault, they spoke ; if not, he read on." When a portion had thus been finished by any company, it was to be sent to the rest for their examination: and they were required, if they felt a doubt about any of the renderings, or could suggest an improvement, to state such doubt or improvement, and the reasons on which it was founded, to the company who had executed the portion. If the alteration were approved, it was to be adopted at once ; if not approved, it was to be referred to a committee of final revisers. While the labor was great, correctness was likely to be secured by this plan : for every portion would first be translated by each member of the party to whom it was assigned ; then considered by them all ; then examined by the other companies ; and then finally revised by the select committee appointed to complete the work : thus, after its first translation, passing through a number of ordeals, varying from thirteen to sixteen, according to the number of persons in the company to which it belonged.

When the revisers had finished their work, a copy was sent to London, where two from each place of meeting, Cambridge, Oxford, and Westminster, six in all, gave another revision ; Andrew Downes, fellow of St. John's College, and the king's Greek professor at Cambridge, and Mr. John Bois, were sent from Cambridge; who the other four were, we have no means of knowing.

After this Bishop Bilson of Winchester and Dr. Miles Smith, of the Oxford company, gave it a final revision, and superintended the work as it passed through the press. Dr. Smith wrote the Preface, which is entitled, "The Translators to the Reader."

The work was given to the public in 1611, in a folio volume, printed in black letter. The marginal references to parallel passages at first were comparatively scanty. In the Old Testament there were 6,588, and in the New 1,517, making a total of 8,105. In subsequent editions others were added, until the edition of 1769, at Oxford, had 64,983.

In the fifth edition of Bishop Horne's Introduction we find the following:

"In 1683 this translation was corrected, and many references to parallel texts were added by Dr. Scattergood; and in 1700, a very fine edition was published in large folio, under the direction of Dr. Tenison, archbishop of Canterbury, with chronological dates, and an index by Bishop Lloyd, and accurate tables of Scripture weights and measures by Bishop Cumberland; but this edition is said to abound with typographical errors. The latest and most complete revision is that made by the late Rev. Dr. Blayney, under the direction of the vice-chancellor and delegates of the Clarendon press at Oxford. In this edition, which was printed both in quarto and folio, in 1769, the punctuation was thoroughly revised; the words printed in Italics were examined and corrected by the Hebrew and Greek originals; the proper names, to the etymology of which allusions are made in the text, were translated and entered in the margin, the summaries of chapters, and running titles at the top of each page corrected; some material errors in the chronology rectified; and the marginal references were reëxamined and corrected, and 30,495 new references were inserted in the margin. From the singular pains bestowed in order to render this edition as accurate as possible, it has hitherto been considered as the standard condition from which all subsequent impressions have been executed. Notwithstanding, however, the great labor and attention bestowed by Dr. Blayney, his edition must now yield the palm of accuracy to the very beautiful and correct edition published by Messrs. Eyre and Strahan, his majesty's printers (but printed by Mr. Woodfall), in 1806, and again in 1813, in quarto; as not fewer than one hundred and sixteen errors were discovered in collating the edition of 1806 with Dr. Blayney's; and one of these errors was an omission of considerable importance. Messrs. Eyre and Strahan's editions may therefore be regarded as approaching as near as possible to what Bibliographers term an immaculate text. Only one erratum, we believe, has been discovered in the edition of 1806. The following particulars relative to the above-mentioned London editions of the Bible may not be unacceptable to the Bibliographical reader; at the same time they will show that their claims to be considered as standard editions are not altogether unfounded. The booksellers of the metropolis, having applied to his majesty's printers to undertake a handsome edition of the Bible, confided the execution of it to Mr. George Woodfall, in 1804. The copy printed from was the current Cambridge edition, with which Mr. W.'s edition agrees page for page. It was afterwards read twice by the Oxford impression then in use, and the proofs were transmitted to the Rev. Launcelot Sharpe, by whom they were read with Dr. Blayney's 4to edition of 1769. After the proofs returned by Mr. S. for press had been corrected, the forms were placed upon the press at which they were to be worked, and another proof was taken. This was read by Mr. Woodfall's superintendent, and afterwards by Mr. W. himself, with Dr. Blayney's edition, and any errors that had previously escaped were corrected; the forms not having been removed from the press after the last proofs had been taken off. By this precaution they avoided the danger of errors (a danger of very frequent occurrence, and of no small magnitude) arising from the removal of the forms from the proof-press to the presses on which the sheets were finally worked off. Of this edition, which was ready for publication in 1806, five hundred copies were printed on imperial 4to, two thousand on royal, and three thousand on medium quarto size. In the course of printing this edition from the Cambridge copy, a great number of very gross errors was discovered in the latter; and the errors in the common Oxford editions above noticed were not so few as twelve hundred! The London edition of 1806 being exhausted, a new impression was put to press in 1810, which was completed with equal beauty and accuracy in 1812, and published in 1813."

In 1847 the American Bible Society appointed a committee of seven to prepare a collated edition of the Bible, which should be as nearly accurate as it could be made in every respect. They finished their work in 1851, and the Board of Managers adopted it, and began using it as their standard. The most accurate edition, in all respects, of the Authorized Version ever published is the one issued from the Cambridge press in 1873, under the editorship of the Rev. F. H. Scrivener, LL. D.

CHAPTER X.

THE REVISED VERSION OF 1881.

For many years Biblical scholars were asking for a new revision of the Scriptures; the faithful labors of the translators of the Authorized Version were duly appreciated; it was the nearest approach to the original text that had ever been given in the English language. Many errors, however, remained in that version, both in the text and in the renderings. It could not be otherwise. Their grammars and lexicons, Hebrew, Greek, and English, were very imperfect; hence the confusion of modes and tenses, and improper renderings, and also the wrong use of prepositions, the article, and erroneous orthography. They had but imperfect and untrustworthy versions to rely upon; and the only manuscript in their possession, dating earlier then the tenth century, was the Codex of Beza, supposed to belong to the sixth century, and containing only the Gospels and the Acts of the Apostles, and a few verses from the third Epistle of John. With all these difficulties in their way, King James' revisers completed their work in about two years and a half.

In February of 1870 both Houses of Convocation of Canterbury unanimously passed a resolution appointing a committee, to confer with a similar committee to be appointed by the convocation of York, to report on the desirableness of a revision of the Authorized Version of the Bible. The Convocation of York refused to act in the matter, and the committee appointed by the Convocation of Canterbury acted by themselves, and in May presented a report recommending a revision. Acting on this report the Convocation appointed a committee of eight members of each house to undertake the work of revision, with the privilege of inviting "the coöperation of any eminent for scholarship, to whatever nation or religious body they belong."

This committee met May 25, 1870, Dr. Samuel Wilberforce, Bishop of Winchester, presiding. The following fundamental rules were adopted on which the revision was to be made:

"*Resolved*, 1. That the committee appointed by the convocation of Canterbury at its last session separate itself into two companies, the one for the revision of the Authorized Version of the Old Testament, the other for the revision of the Authorized Version of the New Testament.

"2. That the company for the revision of the Authorized Version of the Old Testament consist of the bishops of St. David's, Llandoff, Ely and Bath and Wells, and of the following members from the lower house: Archdeacon Rose, Canon Selwyn, Dr. Jebb, and Dr. Kay.

"3. That the company for the revision of the Authorized Version of the New Testament consist of the bishops of Winchester, Gloucester, Bristol, and Salisbury, and of the following members from the lower house: the Prolocutor, the deans of Canterbury and Westminster, and Canon Blakesley.

NOTE.—The Committee sent invitations to a number of the most eminent Hebrew and Greek scholars to unite with them in the work. A number accepted the invitation, and the committee finally consisted of the following:

Old Testament Company.

Bishop E. H. Browne, D. D., of Winchester (chairman).
Professor W. A. Wright, Cambridge (secretary).
W. L. Alexander, D. D.
R. L. Bensly, Esq.
Prof. I. Birrell.
F. Chance, M. D.
T. Chenery, Esq.
Rev. T. K. Cheyne.
Prof. A. B. Davidson, D. D.
Prof. G. Douglas, D. D.
S. R. Drines.
Rev. C. J. Eliott.
F. Field, LL. D.
Prof. I. D. Geden.
C. D. Ginsburg, LL. D.
Canon B. Harrison, A. M.
Canon Lord A. C. Hervey, D.D.
W. Kay, D. D.
S. Leathes, B. D.
Rev. J. R. Lumby.
A. Ollivant, D. D.
Dean, J. J. S. Peroune.
Rev. A. H. Sayce.
Dean R. P. Smith, D. D.
Prof. W. R. Smith.

New Testament Company.

Bishop C. J. Ellicott, D. D., of Gloucester and Bristol (chairman).
Rev. J. Troutbeck, Westminster (secretary).
J. Angus, D. D.
Dean E. H. Bickersteth, D. D.
Dean J. W. Blakesly, D. D.
D. Brown, D. D.
F. J. A. Hurt, D. D.
Rev. W. G. Humphrey.
Canon B. H. Kennedy, D. D.
Archdeacon W. Lee, D. D.
Bishop J. B. Lightfoot, D. D.
W. Milligan, D. D.
Bishop G. Moherly.
W. F. Moulton, D. D.
S. Nenth, D. D.
Archdeacon E. Palmer, D. D.
A. Roberts, D. D.
R. Scott, D. D.
Prebendary F. H. A. Scrivener, LL. D.
G. V. Smith, D. D.
A. P. Stnaley, D. D.
Archbishop R. C. Trench, D.D.
C. J. Vaughan, D. D.
Canon B. F. Wescott, D. D.
Bishop C. Wordsworth, D. C. L.

"4. That the first portion of the work to be undertaken by the Old Testament Company be the revision of the Authorized Version of the Pentateuch.

"5. That the first portion of the work to be undertaken by the New Testament Company be the revision of the Authorized Version of the Synoptical Gospels."

The following principles were laid down to direct the revisers:—

1. To introduce as few alterations as possible into the text of the Authorized Version consistently with faithfulness.

2. To limit, as far as possible, the expression of such alterations to the language of the Authorized and earlier versions.

3. Each company to go twice over the portion to be revised, once provisionally, the second time finally, and on principles of voting as hereinafter is provided.

4. That the text to be adopted be that for which the evidence is decidedly preponderating, and that when the text so adopted differs from that from which the Authorized Version was made, the alteration be indicated in the margin.

5. To make or retain no change in the text, on the second final revision by each company, except two-thirds of those present approve of the same; but on the first revision to decide by simple majorities.

6. In every case of proposed alteration that may have given rise to discussion, to defer the voting thereupon till the next meeting, whensoever the same shall be required by one-third of those present at the meeting, such intended vote to be announced in the notice for the next meeting.

7. To revise the headings of chapters, pages, paragraphs, italics, and punctuation.

8. To refer on the part of each company, when considered desirable, to divines, scholars, and literary men, whether at home or abroad, for their opinions.

9. That the work of each company be communicated to the other as it is completed, in order that there may be as little deviation from uniformity in language as possible.

These two companies held their first session in the Jerusalem Chamber, of Westminster Abbey, June 22, 1870. In August, 1870, Dr. Joseph Angus, president of Regents Park College, London, one of the revisers, arrived in New York with a letter from Bishop Ellicott, chairman of the British New Testament Company, authorizing and inviting Dr. Phillip Schaff, of Union Theological Seminary, New York, to take steps to organize an American revision committee, to coöperate with the British committee.

Dr. Schaff called a meeting, to be held at the Bible House, New York, December 7, 1871, for the purpose of organizing such a committee. A number of eminent scholars were present, Professor Henry B. Smith acted as chairman, and Professor George E. Day as secretary. The following were then appointed:

Old Testament Company.

W. H. Green, D. D., LL. D., Princeton, N. Y. (chairman).
Prof. Geo. E. Day, D. D., New Haven, Conn. (secretary).
C. A. Aiken, D. D.
T. W. Chambers, D. D.
Prof. J. De Witt, D. D.
Prof. G. E. Hare, D. D., LL.D.
Prof. C. P. Krauth, D. D., LL. D.
Prof. C. M. Mead, Ph. D.
Prof. H. Osgood, D. D.
Prof. J. Packard, D. D.
Prof. James Strong, S. T. D., LL. D.

New Testament Company.

T. D. Woolsey, D. D., LL. D., New Haven, (chairman).
Prof. J. H. Thayer, D. D., Andover, Mass. (secretary).
Philip Schaff, D. D., LL. D. (President of the American Committee).
Prof. Ezra Abbot, D. D., LL.D.
T. K. Burr, D. D.
T. Chase, LL. D.
H. Crosby, D. D., LL. D.
Prof. T. Dwight, D. D.
Prof. A. C. Kendrick, D. D., LL. D.
Bishop Alfred Lee, D. D.
Prof. M. B. Riddle, D. D.
Prof. C. Short, LL. D.
E. A. Washburn, D. D.

These companies held their first meeting for work on October 4, 1872.

These committees had many more resources at their command than the revisers of the King James' version. They had all the material possessed by the committee of 1611 in their revision, and in addition they had the *Codex Vaticanus*, which is considered the best manuscript of the New Testament. It is supposed to belong to the fourth century. It contains the New Testament entire to Hebrews 9 : 14, and the rest of the New Testament was added about the fifteenth century, chiefly from the vulgate. They also possessed the *Alexandrian* manuscript, which scholars agree should be dated in the fifth century. This was the first of all the really valuable manuscripts discovered and used in Biblical criticism. It contains the Septuagint and the book of Revelation entire, which so often was mutilated by being at the end of the manuscript. They also had the *Ephræm* manuscript, also belonging to the fifth century. This manuscript is what is called a *Palimpsert*, *i. e.* one writing over another on the same parchment, and the scared writings, which were beneath the writings of Ephræm, were not discovered for a long time, when, by the application of chemicals, the lines of the first writer appeared. It contains parts of the Septuagint, and portions of each book of the New Testament. They had also the *Sinaitic* manuscript, which is the only manuscript copy of the entire New Testament.

Besides the above-mentioned, they had a number of old manuscripts not in possession of the revisers of 1611. They had also the results of all the recent explorations in Bible lands, all the benefits of latest knowledge of languages, and the discoveries in paleography. We have a right to expect a much more correct translation from the originals.

The revsied New Testament was published, simultaneously in England and America, on May 17, 1881; ten years and half was given to the revision, which will speak for the thoroughness of the work, when compared with the two and a half years' work on the Authorized Version. It is expected that the Old Testament will be published during the later part of this year (1884), after over thirteen years of labor.

APPENDIX.

NOTES ON THE OLD TESTAMENT.

The Bible, as the title of the collected books of the Old and New Testaments, is not found earlier than the fifth century. In the New Testament occur the terms, "The Scripture" (Acts 8 : 32; Gal. 3 : 22; 2 Tim. 3 : 16; James 4 : 5), "The Scriptures" (Matt. 21 : 42; Luke 24 : 27), "The Holy Scriptures" (2 Tim. 3 : 15), applied to the Old Testament; and also "Moses and the Law" (Acts 15 : 5 : 21), "Moses and the Prophets" (Luke 16 : 31), as the sacred books read in the synagogues on the Sabbath-day. A distinction is also made between the "Old" and the "New" Covenant (Heb. 7 : 22; 8 : 6; 9 : 15), which gradually led to the extension of the former name to the whole books of the Hebrew Scriptures, and of the latter to those of the Christian Canon. Of "Covenant" the Latin "Testamentum" is the equivalent, and has passed into our phraseology. As MSS. read in the synagogues, and afterwards in churches, were kept in some repository within the sacred edifice, they would naturally be called by the priests, who had charge of them, "*the* Books;" so the Greek word for *book* ($\beta i\beta\lambda o\varsigma$, *biblos*) became naturalized in the various Western languages, as the title of this sacred compilation. It is not, however, found in Anglo-Saxon, though "Gospel," the happy equivalent, good tidings, has come to us from that tongue.

APPENDIX.

DIVISIONS OF THE BIBLE. The Hebrews divided their Scriptures into three parts :—

I. "THE LAW" (Acts 15 : 5, 21) comprising the five books of Moses.

II. "THE PROPHETS" (John 1 : 45) containing the books of Joshua, Judges, I. and II. Samuel, I. and II. Kings, Isaiah, Jeremiah, Ezekiel, and the twelve Minor Prophets.

III. "THE SCRIPTURES" (John 5 : 39). The Poetical or Devotional Books, including :

a. Job, Psalms, Proverbs.

b. Song of Solomon, Ruth, Lamentations, Ecclesiastes, Esther.

c. Daniel, Ezra, Nehemiah, I. and II. Chronicles.

I. THE LAW (*Pentateuch*, i. e. Five Books). The existence of a book bearing this title is traceable to the time of its compilation (Deut. 31 : 24, 26 ; Josh. 1 : 8 ; 8 : 34 ; 24 : 26). The distinctness of the five portions shows they were designed to be separate, and so distinct names were found for each. The Hebrews marked them by the *initial* or *chief* word in the first verse of each ; while in the LXX. they are denoted by words expressing the *subject-matter*, which latter titles have come down to us, e. g. Genesis, Exodus, &c.

II. THE PROPHETS. This general appellation was given to these twenty-one books, because they were *written by* Prophets, who, as the Teachers of the people, were naturally the *annalists* also : e. g. Samuel, Nathan, Gad, Iddo, Isaiah, Jeremiah, &c. Living in communities they became a "caste," who cultivated literature, music, psalmody, &c. ; and their writings (whether devotional or historic) were regarded as more or less *prophetic* (which means *instructive*, as well as *predictive*, Acts 13 : 1 ; 1 Cor. 13 : 2, 8). They were divided into Priores (Joshua, Judges, I. and II. Samuel, I. and II. Kings) and Posteriores ; the latter being subdivided into *Majores* and *Minores*. The former designation was given to the writings of Isaiah, Jeremiah and Ezekiel, because of their *greater bulk*, as well as prophetical prominence. The Book of Daniel was excluded, partly owing to his having exercised no prophetic *office* amongst "the people," partly to its late reception into the Sacred Canon ; and also, in later times, because it was quoted by Christians against the Jews.

III. THE SCRIPTURES (*Kethubim*) include the remaining books of the Hebrew Canon. The first group (*a*) were the devotional books used in the services of the synagogue (the Psalms and Proverbs weekly, Job on the great fasts). The second (*b*) called the "Five Rolls," formed the "Lessons" on special festivals ; the third (*c*) was an Appendix, in which were placed those Canonical books which were not ranked amongst "The Prophets."

DIVISIONS OF THE BOOKS. The quotations made in the New Testament from the Old, cite only the *book* (Acts 2 : 16) from whence they are taken (excepting the Psalms, e. g. Acts 13 : 33, 35). They are mostly from the books read in the synagogue every Sabbath-day, of which there are indications of divisions into sections (Acts 13 : 33, 35 ; Luke 4 : 17 ; Acts 13 : 15 ; 15 : 21 ; 2 Cor. 3 : 14).

The Talmud divided "The Law" into fifty-four portions, one for each Sabbath of the intercalary year. These were called *Parshioth*, which were subdivided "*Lesser Parshioth*," being the sections of the Lesson taken by each individual Reader. These, again, were classed under two heads, viz. "Open" (*Petuchoth*), which marked a change of subject, like the modern paragraph, and began with a *fresh line* in the MSS.; and "Shut" (*Satumoth*), corresponding to minor divisions, like sentences, marked only by a *space* in the line. These breaks in the text were denoted by the initials "P" or "S" in the margin, to catch the Reader's eye: which would seem to be the origin of the ¶ placed before certain verses in the authorized version.

"The Prophets" are quoted in the New Testament as a distinct "book" (Acts 7 : 42); but were also subdivided into Sabbath Lessons, though not with the same precision or authority. These portions were called "Haphtaroth" (*dismissal*, because they were read immediately before the close of the service). These were in the ninth century A. D. subdivided by the Masoretes into verses (*Pesukim*), the termination of each in the Hebrew MSS. being marked by a colon (:), which is retained in the Prayer Book version of the Psalms to point them for chanting. In the thirteenth century a more systematic division (ascribed to Archbishop Langton) were generally adopted to facilitate reference to the text. This combined Cardinal Hugo's division into *Capitula* (which is still retained in our "Chapters,") and the Masoretic division into verses; but it has no further importance.

DIVISIONS OF THE ENGLISH BIBLE. The books in our Old Testament are conveniently arranged according to their subject-matter, thus: I. The Pentateuch (or Five Books of Moses). II. The Historical Books (from Joshua to the end of Esther). III. The Poetical or Devotional Books (from Job to the Song of Solomon). IV. The Prophetical (from Isaiah to Malachi).

THE CANON OF SCRIPTURE. *Canon* (Greek, a *straight rod*), used figuratively of a *testing rule* in art, logic, grammar, or ethics, occurs in the sense of a "rule of life" (Gal. 6 : 16 ; Phil. 3 : 16), and as a *gauge* of excellence (2 Cor. 10 : 13, 16). In the early age of Christianity, the term was used generally to denote a standard of opinion and practice. Its first direct application to the Holy Scriptures occurs in the imprimatur appended by Amphilochius to his Catalogue (A. D. 380). From the time of Origen it has been applied to those books which Christians regard as genuine and of Divine authority. *Uncanonical* are those not specified in the Canon. *Apocryphal* are those supposed to occupy an intermediate position : only useful historically, and as affording "instruction of manners ;" but then valuable only so far as they exemplify the spirit and precepts of the Gospel. External and internal evidence are alike against their inspiration and Divine authority, and they are no part of the rule of faith. The Bible is *the* Canon, or authoritative standard of religion and morals.

THE JEWISH CANON. Before the Captivity there are only faint traces of the preservation of the sacred writings. Moses ordered "the book of the law" to be put "in the side of the ark" (Deut. 31 : 26 ; cf. 2 Kings 22 : 8). To this was subsequently added that of Joshua and other annals; and later, Proverbs, and some Prophecies, for Daniel refers to the "Books" (9 : 2), Zechariah to "the Law and former Prophets" (7 : 12), and Isaiah to "the Book of the Lord" (29 : 18 ; 34 : 16). Ezra and the "Great Synagogue" most probably determined the Canon of the Law in its final shape : and Nehemiah "gathered together the acts of the kings and the prophets, and those of David," when "founding a library" for the second temple (2 Macc. 2: 13). The first notice of the "Old Testament," as a distinct compilation, is in the "Prologue" of the Greek translation of "Ecclesiasticus" (B. C. 131), which specifies the "Law, Prophets, and the rest of *the* books." (Cp. Luke 24: 44; Acts 26: 22). Josephus enumerates twenty-two books as "divine;" viz. *five* of Moses, *thirteen* of Prophets (in which Job was probably included), and *four* "hymns and directions of life." He speaks of all the books of the Old Testament as Canonical, except Job, Proverbs, Ecclesiastes, and Song of Solomon, none of which furnished any materials for his work. They are all quoted in the New Testament as "Scripture," except Judges, Ecclesiastes, Song of Solomon, Esther, Ezra, and Nehemiah; but, in addition, the "Book of Enoch" is quoted by Jude (ver. 14). Our Lord also quotes from an unknown book (Luke 11: 49–51; John 7: 38), and so, too, James (4: 5, 6). Jerome notices that the twenty-two books coincide with the letters in the Hebrew alphabet, and that the five double letters coincide with the five double books (Samuel, Kings, Chronicles, Ezra, and Jeremiah). He gives the contents of the Law, Prophets, and Hagiographa in exact accordance with that of the Hebrew authorities, as mentioned above, classing Daniel with the last. The Talmud also agrees with the same, and gives the writers of each.

PRESERVATION OF THE OLD TESTAMENT. The "Book of the Law," placed by Moses in the side of the ark in the tabernacle (Deut. 31: 26) with the various "Annals" and prophetic books from Joshua to David, Solomon deposited in the temple, where they remained till its destruction (2 Kings 22: 8; Isa. 34: 16).

Daniel had a copy of "the Books" in Babylon (Dan. 9: 2, 11), and also of "Jeremiah" (9: 2). After the temple was rebuilt, Nehemiah collected the sacred books and made "a library" of them (2 Macc. 2: 13), to which were added the writings of Ezra and his contemporaries (Nehemiah, and the later prophets).

THE CHRISTIAN CANON. The books of the Jewish Canon were read from the first in Christian assemblies, as of Divine authority, and were largely quoted by ecclesiastical authors. Between A. D. 200 and 400, fifteen Catalogues of Canonical Books were published. Six of these agree with our present Canon, and three omit only the Book of Revelation. The Canon of Muratori (a fragment written in the middle of the second century, found at Milan) is not a formal catalogue, but it incidentally mentions as Canonical all the books of the New Testament, as received by us, except the Epistles of James and Peter, and that to the Hebrews.

NOTES ON THE NEW TESTAMENT.

EARLY COPIES. There is no existing original MS. of the New Testament written in the first three centuries. The first witnesses to the apostolic text are the early Syriac *Peshito* (Cent. i.) and Latin (Cent. ii.) versions and the rich quotations of Clement of Alexandria (A. D. 220) and of Origen (A. D. 184–254). The most important early MSS. of the New Testament are the following :

SINAITIC (Cent. iv.), in the *Library of St. Petersburg*, found by Tischendorf in the convent of St. Catherine, Mount Sinai, in 1859. The New Testament is entire, with the Epistle of St. Barnabas and part of the "Shepherd of Hermas."

A. ALEXANDRINE (the first half of Cent. v.), in the *Library of the British Museum*, given by Cyril Lucas, patriarch of Constantinople, to Charles I. in 1628. It contained the entire Bible in Greek, with the addition of the Epistles of Clement; but there are some parts of the New Testament missing (St. Matt. 1–25 : 6; St. John 6 : 50; 8 : 52; 2 Cor. 4 : 13; 12 : 6).

B. VATICAN (supposed to be of Cent. iv.), in the *Vatican Library* ever since its foundation, A. D. 1450. It is a MS. of the entire Greek Bible, as far as Heb. 9 : 14, the remainder being added in Cent. xv.

C. ST. EPHREM'S (supposed to be written in the early part of Cent. v.), now in the *Library of Paris*. It was brought from the East to Florence early in Cent. xvi., and came to Paris with Catherine de Medicis in the middle of that century. It contains fragments of the LXX. and of each book of the New Testament. In Cent. xii. the original writing was effaced, and some Greek writings of "Ephrem Syrus" were written over it.

D. BEZA's (Cent. vi.), found by Beza in the monastery of St. Irenæus at Lyons, A. D. 1562, and presented by him to the *University Library, Cambridge*. It is a Græco-Latin MS. of the Gospels and Acts, with small fragments of Epistles of St. John. It abounds in interpolations, especially in the Acts of the Apostles.

L. PARISIAN IMPERIAL (Cent. viii.), one of the most important of the late Uncial MSS. It contains the four Gospels (except St. Matt. 4 : 22; 5 : 14.; 28 : 17–20; St. Mark 10 : 16–20; 15 : 2–20; St. John 21 : 15–

25). It agrees in a remarkable manner with the quotations of Origen and with MS. B.

List of New Testament MSS. :

Uncial.—Gospels, 34; Acts and Catholic Epistles, 10; St. Paul's Epistles 14; Evangelistaria, 58.

Cursive.—Gospels, 601; Acts and Catholic Epistles, 229: St. Paul's Epistles, 283; Evangelistaria, 183.

The NEW TESTAMENT is the sacred Scripture of the last dispensation, in which a New Covenant is made between God and man, by which *all mankind* are offered the privileges of (1) *adoption* to be the son of God, (2) *incorporation* into Christ's Church, (3) *inheritance* in the kingdom of heaven. As no preference is given to any particular family or people, but these privileges are freely offered to all, the *offer*, the incorporated *society* who accept it, the *faith* (or terms of membership), are all said to be *catholic*, or universal—viz., *open* to all, not necessarily *accepted* by all. This offer is called the Gospel (*good tidings*), the Preacher of which is Christ, the Head also of the society which is called the Church, or "Body of the Lord."

The BOOKS of the NEW TESTAMENT have, to some extent, their counterpart in the Old. Thus, the Four Gospels correspond with the Pentateuch, as they contain an account of the Origin and Law of the Covenant; the Acts of the Apostles with the Historical Books (especially Joshua and Judges); the twenty-one Epistles with the Prophets; and Revelation with the concluding portions of Daniel and Ezekiel.

Divisions of the New Testament

I. Constitutional and Historical.
  i. The Four Gospels: two by Apostles, two by missionary Evangelists.
  ii. The Acts of the Apostles, forming the link of connection between the historical and didactic portions.

II. Didactic.
  i. The Pauline Epistles, viz.:
   a. *Doctrinal*, addressed to churches — viz., Romans, Corinthians, Galatians, Ephesians, Philippians, Colossians, Thessalonians, Hebrews.
   b. *Pastoral*, addressed to suffragan bishops— viz., Timothy and Titus.
   c. *Special*, to an individual (Philemon).
  ii. Catholic Epistles, addressed to the Church at large.
   a. One of St. James.
   b. Two of St. Peter.
   c. Three of St. John.
   d. One of St. Jude.

III. Prophetic. The Revelation of St. John the Divine.

INDEX

	PAGE.
Introductory Chapter,	5
Early Saxon Translations,	8
Wycliffe and his Translations,	16
Tyndale and his Translations,	22
Coverdale and his Translations,	33
Matthew's Bible, and the Great Bible,	37
The Genevan Bible,	44
The Bishop's Bible,	47
The Rheims and Douay Version,	51
The Authorized Version,	53
The Revised Version of 1881,	63
Appendix,	70

www.ingramcontent.com/pod-product-compliance
Lightning Source LLC
Chambersburg PA
CBHW020325090426
42735CB00009B/1402